Edgar C Reed

POB 50296

Fort Myers, FL 33994

ISBN-13: 978-0991534326

ISBN-10: 0991534328

```
[]O[]O[]O[]O[]O[]O []O[]
[]O                    O[]
[]O                    O[]
[]O                    O[]
[]O                    O[]
[]O        GOD         O[]
[]O         IS         O[]
[]O        LOVE        O[]
[]O                    O[]
[]O                    O[]
[]O                    O[]
[]O                    O[]
[]O                    O[]
[]O                    O[]
[]O                    O[]
[]O                    O[]
[]O[]O[]O[]O[]O[]O []O[]
```

Dedicated
To
Evangelist
Barbara Davis Gooden

Love one another for God is
love, and everyone that
practice love pleases God. If
you do not practice LOVE,
you do not know God for he
is love (Holy Bible, 1 John
4:7, 8).

TABLE OF CONTENTS

PSALM 23

A Psalm of David

The LORD is my shepherd, and I shall not want. He makes me to lie down in green pastures. He leads me beside still waters.

He restores my soul. He leads me in the path of righteousness for his name sake. Yea, thou I walk through the valley of the shadow of death, I will fear no evil for thou are with me, thy rod and thy staff they comfort me. Thou prepare a table before me in the presences of my enemies, thou anoint my head with oil, and my cup runs over. Surely goodness and mercy shall follow me all the days of my life, and I will dwell in the house of the LORD forever.

1. Introduction

Psalm 23 historically has been popular amongst many for obvious reasons. However there is hidden power in its words. This power can promote good health within the human body when it becomes ill. It can comfort the battered soul in times of pain and unpleasant days. What Psalm 23 tells us when heard in the human voice is that God is a sensitive caregiver and protector who we, his creation can put our faith in that God loves and delights in consistently meeting our physical and psychological needs. Also it tells us that God loves to meet these needs throughout our existence. However, there is a universal law that must be obeyed to release this wonderful power. The universal law consists of belief. You must believe these words to be true, for in doing so there will grow within you the positive emotions needed to bring forth a powerful radiating healthy perception of LIFE.

In the mind or soul, love flows downward flooding the body with the power of healing that comes from an all loving God to its beloved creation. Love is protecting and caring for others with no expectation of something in return. God designed us to draw strength and power from love. That is why love makes us feel happy, and causes the release of growth and repair chemicals in our body that makes us healthy. Not all will understand this truth, but a few have the gift of understanding that God your caregiver and protector will reveal to you what has been hidden in plain sight. Believe and you can benefit from this hidden power which is not seen but felt. I shall present some scientific research in the area of religious experience that suggests the formation of an improved emotional state within the mind as a result of communion with the divine. You as sheep are capable of evolving beyond sheep and becoming as the shepherd, just as the infant and child are capable of growing beyond infant and child to become as the parent. God's undying love for his creation is beyond the human capacity to fully understand. But we can fully trust that God will consistently meet our daily needs for his loving care and protection. There is the realm of the visible and the invisible world involved in our physical and psychological needs. The body as the visible realm that we can see and the mind and soul as the invisible world that we cannot see has its mysteries. The body that which is visible is being influenced by something, and God has delegated that this realm of the visible be influenced by the invisible world, that which is the soul and mind. Hear the inner voice of the good shepherd instructions, for he speaks to you from within the crown made for righteousness. God dwells in the invisible world, the human soul and mind. The house of God is within the soul and mind, God takes up abode within it. We feel the influence of the emotions of LOVE, FEAR, ANGER, and SADNESS because they spring forth of the soul and mind, and flow like a mighty river into our body. There are the beliefs we have that color our inner world, that causes sickness and death, or release the wings of healing. LOVE, changes our body, and the visible world that is around our body. Love is the quintessence of our

emotions, for God is LOVE.
Therefore, the body is healed,
and in harmony with its
divine creator and protector
who give us unconditional
love, and makes his sun to
rise on the good as well as
the evil, and send his rain on
the unrighteous as well as the
righteous. Love does no ill to
anyone, therefore LOVE
makes possible union with

God (Holy Bible, Proverb 13:10). Belief in a caring and loving God, promotes a happy healthy mind and body, which can bring about healing. If you change your belief and perception of LIFE, you can change the state of health in your body. If you go through life being angry, sad, and fearing, you can have a lot of sickness in your life, and if you go through life feeling love and happiness and having a pleasant and positive attitude you can reduce or eliminate sickness in your life. For God says, if anyone defile the temple (your body) of God, he shall destroy (bring on sickness and death), for the temple or dwelling place of God is made to be HOLY, you were made to practice LOVE because love changes the chemistry of the body to that of good health. God is LOVE (Holy Bible, 1 John 4:8). Psalm 23 has been a powerful source of nourishment for the seeds of hope in many that understood the power behind its words. The feelings that whatever was troubling you are going to turn out alright is medicine to the storms of fear and worry that is battering your mind. With the powerful benefits attributed to this wonderful psalm, no wonder it has been popular for so long amongst many. Psalm 23 words can promote healing when ill, and bring comfort to the hurting soul in times of trouble.

[]⊙[]⊙[]⊙[]⊙[]⊙[]⊙ []⊙[]
[]⊙   ⊙[]
[]⊙   ⊙[]
[]⊙   ⊙[]
[]⊙   ⊙[]
[]⊙   LOVE   ⊙[]
[]⊙   YOUR   ⊙[]
[]⊙   SELF   ⊙[]
[]⊙   ⊙[]
[]⊙   ⊙[]
[]⊙   ⊙[]
[]⊙   ⊙[]
[]⊙   ⊙[]
[]⊙   ⊙[]
[]⊙   ⊙[]
[]⊙   ⊙[]
[]⊙[]⊙[]⊙[]⊙[]⊙[]⊙ []⊙[]

2. The Good Shepherd

We your people are the sheep of your pastures (Holy Bible, Psalm 79:13). The good shepherd is seen as up early in the morning before the sun rise, preparing to take the sheep to still waters and green pastures. He prepares the sheep dog for the long hard day, of herding the sheep through the uncertain path of hidden danger. With hope of not losing any sheep along the way, he sounds his sheep dog whistle and the dog obeys, moving the sheep forward to his commands. When the good shepherd want the sheep to go left he sounds his whistle and the sheep dog move to the sheep right getting the sheep to go left. When he want the sheep to go right he sounds his whistle and the sheep dog move to the sheep left getting the sheep to go right. When the sheep has arrived at the still water and green pasture, they are allowed to drink and eat their fill. The good shepherd ever watching his sheep close for those that may stray and fall prey to predators, because the valley of the shadow of death is ever near. When the sheep have eating and drunk their fill, the good shepherd sounds his whistle and the sheep dog obey and herd the sheep back to the barn to keep them safe from the dangers of the night. He sounds his sheep dog whistle and the dog obeys, moving the sheep forward to his command. He sounds his whistle and the sheep dog move to the right of the sheep getting the sheep to go left. He sounds his whistle and the sheep dog move to the left of the sheep getting the sheep to go right. And when the good shepherd gets the flock to the safety of the barn, he herds them inside and they are safe throughout the night. God cares for his flock, and has protected his creation since the beginning of the world. Since God gave the wonderful gift of his Sun, everything within the visible realm has been made for our physical existence. Moon, stars, and the heavens, these are gifts from God to us to light the way in times of darkness. God made us, and we are the sheep of his pasture (Holy Bible, Psalm 100:3). Like sheep we may go astray, but God's staff reaches out to us, to steer us back on the righteous path. The good shepherd is LOVE, which makes his house in the mind and soul. It is the sheep dog whistle that sends out the command to the sheep dog. The sheep dog changes directions and the sheep responds. The sheep dog represents the body changing its biology either by causing bad or good chemistry to flood the body. The body like the sheep responds to this chemistry change in either producing sickness or good health in your life. God feeds his flock, gather the lambs with his arms, carry them in his bosom, and lead the young (Holy Bible, Isaiah 40:11). We love the good feelings that wells up inside of us, that a sensitive and responsive God can give us. From the laying of the foundation of the world, God's love for his creation (you) has been unsurpassed. Everyone and everything deserves LOVE. In the beginning there truly was darkness. But, it is not the darkness that you know. Remember, the light you see is only a small portion of the ALL, a form of radiant energy. This energy engulfs all, and is all. God caused the gas and dust of the cold darkness to come together under immense pressure that the union of such transformed it into light. In doing so our caregiver and protector God gave a gift of LOVE so that we may see beauty in the many things he gave us. God satisfied our physical and psychological needs in the formation of a world to cradle and nurture our existence. God gave the gift of green pastures, and has set us down in the midst of them.

God's sun gives life and can take it away; therefore God surrounds us with his shield which is generated within the depths of the earth. Love God for he loves you forever.

```
[]⊙[]⊙[]⊙[]⊙[]⊙[]⊙ []⊙[]
[]⊙                    ⊙[]
[]⊙                    ⊙[]
[]⊙                    ⊙[]
[]⊙                    ⊙[]
[]⊙        LOVE        ⊙[]
[]⊙       OTHERS       ⊙[]
[]⊙         AS         ⊙[]
[]⊙        YOU         ⊙[]
[]⊙        LOVE        ⊙[]
[]⊙        YOUR        ⊙[]
[]⊙        SELF        ⊙[]
[]⊙                    ⊙[]
[]⊙                    ⊙[]
[]⊙                    ⊙[]
[]⊙                    ⊙[]
[]⊙[]⊙[]⊙[]⊙[]⊙[]⊙ []⊙[]
```

3. Green Pastures

God causes the earth to produce green pastures, the herd yielding seed, and the fruit trees with seeds inside their fruit (Holy Bible, Genesis 1:11). The grass is beautiful and green, relaxing and calming in its color as far as the eye can see. Just the right height for lying down in, and not feeling smothered in the growth. The sky is a pretty blue, speckled with white puffy clouds that give relief from the sun. God causes the green pastures to grow for his creation so that they have food from the earth (Holy Bible, Psalm 104:14).

[]⊙[]⊙[]⊙[]⊙[]⊙[]⊙ []⊙[]
[]⊙ ⊙[]
[]⊙ ⊙[]
[]⊙ ⊙[]
[]⊙ ⊙[]
[]⊙ LIFE ⊙[]
[]⊙ IS ⊙[]
[]⊙ WHAT ⊙[]
[]⊙ YOU ⊙[]
[]⊙ MAKE ⊙[]
[]⊙ IT ⊙[]
[]⊙ ⊙[]
[]⊙ ⊙[]
[]⊙ ⊙[]
[]⊙ ⊙[]
[]⊙ ⊙[]
[]⊙[]⊙[]⊙[]⊙[]⊙[]⊙ []⊙[]

4. He Restores My Soul

In times of unpleasant circumstances we instinctively want to act the way we feel, however, acting the way we feel is not always the Godly thing to do. An angry soul and mind makes us want to hurt those that anger us, either physically or psychologically. But, modeling the behavior of God our caregiver and protector, the architect of LOVE, restores our mind and soul to righteousness. Meditate daily yea believers on the love of the father our God, and seek insight into love and its power to heal the sicken body, and broken hearted mind and soul.

```
[]⊙[]⊙[]⊙[]⊙[]⊙[]⊙ []⊙[]
[]⊙                    ⊙[]
[]⊙                    ⊙[]
[]⊙                    ⊙[]
[]⊙                    ⊙[]
[]⊙        GIVE        ⊙[]
[]⊙        LOVE        ⊙[]
[]⊙        AND         ⊙[]
[]⊙        YOU         ⊙[]
[]⊙        WILL        ⊙[]
[]⊙         BE         ⊙[]
[]⊙       LOVED        ⊙[]
[]⊙                    ⊙[]
[]⊙                    ⊙[]
[]⊙                    ⊙[]
[]⊙                    ⊙[]
[]⊙[]⊙[]⊙[]⊙[]⊙[]⊙ []⊙[]
```

GIVE
LOVE
AND
YOU
WILL
BE
LOVED

5. Path of Righteousness

We are always in danger of leaving the path and being led astray from the path of righteousness. Temptation is ever present to pull us from the right path, and out onto the dangerous path that leads us through the valley of the shadow of death. The path of righteousness earns us the crown of LIFE (Holy Bible, James 1:12). The path of unrighteousness leads to sickness, sadness and death. Don't use your body for unrighteousness; it was made to be righteous for God to dwell (Holy Bible, Roman 6:13). You were created to serve a better and higher purpose with this gift of LIFE.

```
[]⊙[]⊙[]⊙[]⊙[]⊙[]⊙ []⊙[]
[]⊙                    ⊙[]
[]⊙                    ⊙[]
[]⊙                    ⊙[]
[]⊙                    ⊙[]
[]⊙        THERE       ⊙[]
[]⊙         IS         ⊙[]
[]⊙       HEALING      ⊙[]
[]⊙         IN         ⊙[]
[]⊙        LOVE        ⊙[]
[]⊙                    ⊙[]
[]⊙                    ⊙[]
[]⊙                    ⊙[]
[]⊙                    ⊙[]
[]⊙                    ⊙[]
[]⊙                    ⊙[]
[]⊙[]⊙[]⊙[]⊙[]⊙[]⊙ []⊙[]
```

6. Shadow of Death

How do I live around evil people who at any time can take my LIFE, and I secure happiness for me. Evil stems from mismanagement of our gift of emotions. When we become angry at another the chance or shadow of death is always close and near. Also when we fall prey to sadness, the shadow of death is always close and never far away. But yea, thou I walk through the valley of the shadow of death, I will fear no evil for I know my God is forever with me. Evil people are all around us, ready to still our joy and happiness if we are not careful.

[]O[]O[]O[]O[]O[]O []O[]
[]O   O[]
[]O   O[]
[]O   O[]
[]O   O[]
[]O   LOVE   O[]
[]O   OVERCOMES   O[]
[]O   DEATH   O[]
[]O   O[]
[]O   O[]
[]O   O[]
[]O   O[]
[]O   O[]
[]O   O[]
[]O   O[]
[]O   O[]
[]O[]O[]O[]O[]O[]O []O[]

7. Thou Are With Me

God dwells within the soul and mind so he is with you always. Know you not that you are the temple of God, and that the spirit of God lives within you. (Holy Bible, 1 Corinthians 3:16). We experience GOD in the mind and soul, and he is manifested with our body.

[]⊙[]⊙[]⊙[]⊙[]⊙[]⊙ []⊙[]
[]⊙   ⊙[]
[]⊙   ⊙[]
[]⊙   ⊙[]
[]⊙   ⊙[]
[]⊙   LOVE   ⊙[]
[]⊙   WORKS   ⊙[]
[]⊙   NO   ⊙[]
[]⊙   HURT   ⊙[]
[]⊙   ⊙[]
[]⊙   ⊙[]
[]⊙   ⊙[]
[]⊙   ⊙[]
[]⊙   ⊙[]
[]⊙   ⊙[]
[]⊙   ⊙[]
[]⊙[]⊙[]⊙[]⊙[]⊙[]⊙ []⊙[]

8. Thy Rod and Thy Staff

God is our protector, if we practice righteous living we get in less trouble. The shepherd carries the rod and staff as the tools of his trade. The rod and staff can be used by the shepherd for many things throughout the course of caring for and protecting the sheep. One thing the shepherd uses the rod for is protecting his sheep while traveling through the valley of the shadow of death towards green pastures and still waters. The shepherd must protect them while grazing in the pasture and drinking from the water. David used the rod to protect his father's sheep. David said to Saul, while protecting my father's sheep a loin and a bear took a baby sheep out of the flock. I went after the bear and loin and killed both of them, delivering the sheep out of their mouth (1 Samuel 17:34, 35). The rod also comforts the sheep, because in the hands of God it is seen as their protector. The shepherd staff can be used for a lot of purposes. One purpose it is used for is to grab a sheep and pull it to the shepherd for close inspection for injury, or to pull a sheep to the shepherd to pull a thorn from sheep's foot. God is truly a protector of his flock, and is ready to do battle when we are threatened in life.

```
[]⊙[]⊙[]⊙[]⊙[]⊙[]⊙ []⊙[]
[]⊙                    ⊙[]
[]⊙                    ⊙[]
[]⊙                    ⊙[]
[]⊙                    ⊙[]
[]⊙         THERE      ⊙[]
[]⊙          IS        ⊙[]
[]⊙          NO        ⊙[]
[]⊙         FEAR       ⊙[]
[]⊙          IN        ⊙[]
[]⊙         LOVE       ⊙[]
[]⊙                    ⊙[]
[]⊙                    ⊙[]
[]⊙                    ⊙[]
[]⊙                    ⊙[]
[]⊙                    ⊙[]
[]⊙[]⊙[]⊙[]⊙[]⊙[]⊙ []⊙[]
```

9. The House of the LORD

The house of God is within your mind, which holds the spirit of God (Holy Bible, 1 Corinthians 3:16). God dwells within the crown (head) which holds the mind. When a baby enters the world from its mother's womb, we say it is crowning, because the head come forth first before the rest of the body. The concise Oxford dictionary of current English (2011) defines crown to also mean the "whole head" (p. 198). [1] God live within the mind, you experience him many times when you are about to do something bad, and you are in conflict within your mind whether to do evil or good. You are the living stone built to be a spiritual house, acceptable to God (Holy Bible, 1 Peter 2:5). You are the living temple that has the capacity to practice love and make the world a better place for you and those around you. The house of God is within you, and there he shall dwell.

```
[]⊙[]⊙[]⊙[]⊙[]⊙[]⊙ []⊙[]
[]⊙                    ⊙[]
[]⊙                    ⊙[]
[]⊙                    ⊙[]
[]⊙                    ⊙[]
[]⊙      THERE         ⊙[]
[]⊙       IS           ⊙[]
[]⊙    HAPPINESS       ⊙[]
[]⊙       IN           ⊙[]
[]⊙      LOVE          ⊙[]
[]⊙                    ⊙[]
[]⊙                    ⊙[]
[]⊙                    ⊙[]
[]⊙                    ⊙[]
[]⊙                    ⊙[]
[]⊙                    ⊙[]
[]⊙[]⊙[]⊙[]⊙[]⊙[]⊙ []⊙[]
```

THERE
IS
HAPPINESS
IN
LOVE

10. Mind/ Body Relationship

You have the capacity to use your mind to improve your health, solve your day-to-day problems, and commune with God who dwells within you. Research (Williams, 2012) aimed at understanding how the impact of the mind and emotions upon the body can lead to serious medical illness even death, has found a link between negative emotion and illness in the body. [2]

The words mind and soul in this book has been interchangeable, and when referring to "spirit," "he" or "his," we are referring to God. I would like to think that God has a combination of both qualities; male and female because both have their benefits in the journey through life. This book has NOT weighed you down with theories, and will strive to NOT be technical, but as simplistic as possible. The Greek word psyche can be used to refer to "the mind" and "the soul"

(Rajamanickam, 2007). [3] The mind and soul tells the body what to do, and the body obeys. Our physical and mental health is shaped by the way we think. Many of us do not realize that what we think can hurt or repair our body. Love is a repairer of the body, and fear, anger, and sadness will always hurt your body.

```
[]O[]O[]O[]O[]O[]O []O[]
[]O                    O[]
[]O                    O[]
[]O                    O[]
[]O                    O[]
[]O        THERE       O[]
[]O         IS         O[]
[]O         NO         O[]
[]O       ANGER        O[]
[]O         IN         O[]
[]O        LOVE        O[]
[]O                    O[]
[]O                    O[]
[]O                    O[]
[]O                    O[]
[]O                    O[]
[]O[]O[]O[]O[]O[]O []O[]
```

11. Divine Communion

There is an improved emotional state within the human mind and soul as a result of communing with the divine. Communion with the divine is a special relationship in which you, as good sheep want to stay in close proximity to God. Sheep know there caregiver

and protector voice, and
follow it to stay within close
proximity. God made us
from the dust of the earth
and gave us the gift of life,
and we became a living soul
(Holy Bible, Genesis 2:7).
We that are enlighten share
in common with God the
love of happiness, calmness,
peacefulness, and love of
living untroubled in life. Our

mind and soul is aligned with God's universal mind of love. We can experience love and happiness in our mind without the aid of another person, as well as experiencing it with the aid of another person. Because of the brain's prefrontal cortex we can experience God's beautiful love and the happiness it gives in our head which manifest in our body. The reading of Psalm 23 can give us that cognitive experience of God's beautiful love and the happiness that is associated with it. Happiness and love can be generated in your brain; you just have to want to do it. When we think of God, feel love for God, or when we hear of God's loving attributes, such as in Psalm 23, our brain releases chemicals like oxytocin, growth hormones, other neurotransmitters and a lot more powerful stuff that benefit us in a positive way. Here is the power in the words of Psalm 23 that can attack sickness and improve health. The mind/ body relationship that bring about healing through continued meditation on this powerful psalm. Our beliefs and perceptions of life cause our body harm, or help our body to thrive. Communing with God changes our perceptions of life and helps us to live a happy and fulfilling life.

```
[]O[]O[]O[]O[]O[]O []O[]
[]O                    O[]
[]O                    O[]
[]O                    O[]
[]O                    O[]
[]O        THERE       O[]
[]O          IS        O[]
[]O          NO        O[]
[]O       SADNESS      O[]
[]O          IN        O[]
[]O         LOVE       O[]
[]O                    O[]
[]O                    O[]
[]O                    O[]
[]O                    O[]
[]O                    O[]
[]O[]O[]O[]O[]O[]O []O[]
```

12. Your Needs in Life

For us to live happy and have good health, we will need food, water, shelter, good relationships, and self-actualization. The needs of the body and mind both have to be satisfied to be completely happy. To not do so, causes frustration, anger, disappointment, and sadness.

There is evidence that we need love, and other needs to be met to have a good healthy quality of life. Abraham Maslow hierarchy of needs point out needs must be satisfied in order to avoid feeling bad and overt bad behavior, and John Bowlby attachment theory presents evidence that negative consequences like poor mental health are a result of not getting our need for love satisfied. [4] [5] Not getting our needs satisfied brings on a whole host of negative emotions and feelings. Being in this state of mind for a long time can bring on sickness and even death. The body was not created to live in such a state of NOT having our needs met. God wants our every need to be met (Holy Bible, Philippians 4:19). He wants us to be healthy and not sick; he wants us to have all we need to enjoy a full abundant and happy life. Psalm 23 assures us of this universal truth. Satisfying our physical and psychological needs are important to good health and promoting happiness. You cannot get around this truth, it is as vital to life as the air you breathe. God intended for ALL your wants in life to be satisfied. He gave you freely food, air, water, and anything you needed for a full and happy life. But, it has been man that has hoarded the gifts God freely given you, and has made you suffer and pay for them. Unpleasant events in life do not have to ruin your gift for happiness. Psalm 23 says it all, God made you for happiness, now do what it takes to take back your joy from all the stress and suffering man has put on you. Start by rejecting the life style man has given you, unhealthy foods, stress filled life style, drugs that do not cure sickness but only quiet the symptoms. Take charge of your life and eat healthy, stay away from drugs and alcohol, and anything that has a potential of hurting and harming your body. Remember that your body is the temple of our God, and it has been made to be a holy place.

[]☉[]☉[]☉[]☉[]☉[]☉ []☉[]
[]☉   ☉[]
[]☉   ☉[]
[]☉   ☉[]
[]☉   TO   ☉[]
[]☉   PRACTICE   ☉[]
[]☉   LOVE   ☉[]
[]☉   IS   ☉[]
[]☉   LOVING   ☉[]
[]☉   GOD   ☉[]
[]☉   ☉[]
[]☉   ☉[]
[]☉   ☉[]
[]☉   ☉[]
[]☉   ☉[]
[]☉   ☉[]
[]☉[]☉[]☉[]☉[]☉[]☉ []☉[]

13. The Power of Belief

There is a power in the universe that makes all things possible, and that power is BELIEF. This invisible power dwells within you, and radiates from the mind. This power is greater than any, and makes possible ALL things thought of by the mind. "Therefore I say unto you, what things so ever ye desire, when you pray, believe you have received them, and you shall have them" (Holy Bible, Mark 11:24). What we believe determines how we see the world, for the good or for the worse within it. Belief unleashes forces that take what is in the mind and produce it into the physical world. Everything of man's creation or doing has come into existence through the power of belief. Without belief it is impossible to know God, to experience God which is love you must believe in the power of LOVE, and that love will heal and make you whole and happy.

[]☉[]☉[]☉[]☉[]☉[]☉ []☉[]
[]☉   ☉[]
[]☉   ☉[]
[]☉   ☉[]
[]☉   ☉[]
[]☉   BE   ☉[]
[]☉   LOVERS   ☉[]
[]☉   OF   ☉[]
[]☉   PEACE   ☉[]
[]☉   ☉[]
[]☉   ☉[]
[]☉   ☉[]
[]☉   ☉[]
[]☉   ☉[]
[]☉   ☉[]
[]☉   ☉[]
[]☉[]☉[]☉[]☉[]☉[]☉ []☉[]

14. Attachment

The relationship between God and his creation is an enduring relationship based on LOVE. We were designed to need love, and give love, and will feel a host of negative drawbacks when without love. When we are given love there is a host of positive benefit that comes with love. We are automatically drawn like a magnet to someone that is sensitive and caring. Love is truly what makes the world go around. The world is God's gift to us out of love, and we are to be consistent caregivers and protectors of this wonder gift to us. The love between God and us are enduring.

[]⊙[]⊙[]⊙[]⊙[]⊙[]⊙ []⊙[]
[]⊙   ⊙[]
[]⊙   ⊙[]
[]⊙   ⊙[]
[]⊙   ⊙[]
[]⊙   BLESSED   ⊙[]
[]⊙   ARE   ⊙[]
[]⊙   THEM   ⊙[]
[]⊙   THAT   ⊙[]
[]⊙   LOVE   ⊙[]
[]⊙   ⊙[]
[]⊙   ⊙[]
[]⊙   ⊙[]
[]⊙   ⊙[]
[]⊙   ⊙[]
[]⊙   ⊙[]
[]⊙[]⊙[]⊙[]⊙[]⊙[]⊙ []⊙[]

15. Summary

Change your diet and learn how to cut out a lot of the stress in your life through stress management techniques. Stress is the biggest cause of many of the sickness we are familiar with today. [6] [7] Work to satisfy your physical and psychological needs as long as they do not hurt you or others in the process. Your needs will be shelter, food, happiness, and many other needs that are not mentioned. Regular reading of Psalm 23 words will reverberate in your mind and soul, reassuring you of God's role in your life. Wonderful things will happen in this process of the reading the psalm. Hope which is a life changing emotion will grow like a well nurtured tree in your mind and soul releasing powerful biological chemicals that will flood your body and promote wellbeing. You have a psychological need to be in close proximity to God and will seek out that attachment when threaten with unpleasant situations. There are examples, that in times of sorrow, people who are not believers will call on God for help. There is abundant research indicating that the LOVE and happiness that God represents, can contribute to lowering the morbidity and mortality in older adults. [8]

Reading Psalm 23 to a person who has taken ill can boost their immune system if they are a believer. This is accomplished through the reassurance they get from the words which convey God's role as a caregiver and protector of his creation. Pessimistic thinking during illness can lead to anxiety depression and even death however thinking optimistically can lead to hope and confidence. A God who is perceived as being responsive to our physical and psychological needs can develop within us a feeling of security. You know you can depend of God to be there, even if no one else is there for you during unpleasant times. There is research

(Ong, 2010) suggesting that a change takes place in the human brain when communing with God. This universal mystical union with the divine is associated with positive feelings of love and happiness. Subjects who wanted to have a religious experience were put under neuroimaging, a religious state was experienced when believers was asked to read or recite Psalm 23. This religious experience appeared in neuroimaging data. [9]

You have a psychological need to be in close proximity to God and will seek out that attachment when threaten with unpleasant situations. Psalms 23 assures us of that enduring relationship.

[]O[]O[]O[]O[]O[]O []O[]
[]O   O[]
[]O   O[]
[]O   O[]
[]O   O[]
[]O   LET   O[]
[]O   YOUR   O[]
[]O   LOVE   O[]
[]O   SHINE   O[]
[]O   AS   O[]
[]O   THE   O[]
[]O   SUN   O[]
[]O   O[]
[]O   O[]
[]O   O[]
[]O   O[]
[]O[]O[]O[]O[]O[]O []O[]

16. References

[1] Fowler, H. W., & Fowler, F. G. (2011). The concise Oxford dictionary of current English. Oxford University Press, USA.

[2] Williams, R., & Williams, V. (2012). Anger kills: Seventeen strategies for controlling the hostility that

can harm your health. New York, NY: Time Books, a division of Random House, Inc.

[3] Rajamanickam, M. (2007). Modern general psychology: Thoroughly revised and expanded (vol. 1). Concept Publishing Company, India.

[4] Rakowski, N. (2011). Maslow's hierarchy of needs model . . . Druck und Bindung: Books on Demand Gmbh, Norderstedt Germany.

[5] Holmes, J. (2006). John Bowlby and Attachment Theory. New York, NY: Routledge

[6] Shirey, M. R., McDaniel, A. M., Ebright, P. R., Fisher, M. L., & Doebbeling, B. N. (2010). Understanding nurse manager stress and work complexity: factors that make a difference. Journal of Nursing Administration, 40(2), 82-91.

[7] Steptoe, A., & Kivimäki, M. (2012). Stress and

cardiovascular disease. Nature Reviews Cardiology, 9(6), 360-370.

[8] Ong, A. D. (2010). Pathways linking positive emotion and health in later life. *Current Directions in Psychological Science, 19(6), 358-362.*

[9] McNamara, P. (2009). The neuroscience of religious experience. New York, NY: Cambridge University Press.